CRESCENT CITY
MEMOIRS

From A Poetic View

NATASHA THOMAS

To order additional copies of this book, contact:
Xlibris
844-714-8691
www.Xlibris.com
Orders@Xlibris.com

ISBN: Softcover   978-1-6641-3223-8
         EBook   978-1-6641-3224-5

Library of Congress Control Number: 2020918984

Print information available on the last page

Rev. date: 10/01/2020

CONTENTS

DEDICATION

IN HONOR OF MY PARENTS, WHO HAVE GONE TO BE WITH THE LORD,

IT WAS INSTILLED IN ME TO BE CERTAIN, MY HEART AND MIND WAS ON ONE ACCORD.

MY MOTHER PROMOTED HIGHER EDUCATION, AND
MY DAD WORKED HARD EVERYDAY,

TO ENSURE I HAD WHAT I NEEDED, AND WITH PRAYER THEY MADE A WAY.

I AM GRATEFUL FOR THEIR CONSTANT ENCOURAGEMENT,

SUPPORT AND UNDYING LOVE,

NOW THEY CAN GUIDE ME AS ANGELS, AND SMILE FROM UP ABOVE!

NOSTALGIA AND CULTURE

Strolling the Riverwalk and gazing at the still waters of the
mighty Mississippi, is symbolic of a peaceful joy.

Some watched the riverboats pass, and listened to soothing
sounds of Jazz, as young girls and boys.

Seeing the beautiful Clydesdales, as they trotted along in the fun-filled parades,

listening to the melodious sounds of the High School bands, and enamored
by the beautiful Indian costumes that were handmade.

Visions of art at its finest, were expressed on the soulful streets of the Vieux Carre'.

People sipped on coffee at Café Du monde, and then caught a view
overlooking the city from the top of Jax Brewery.

We heard the shouts of the roaring fans supporting the New Orleans Saints,
and enamored by the mesmerizing Treme' District, with its colorful paint.

We ate snowballs, huckabucks and patronized local corner stores.

Let's not forget Krauss, the shops on Canal Street, the Joy Theatre, Woolworth and more.

Mardi Gras festivities is indeed a sight to see, it is a conglomerate
of art, talent, tradition, and a triumphant jubilee.

From, experiencing Super Sunday, and enjoying the wonderful brass bands,
to the beats of Congo Square to celebrate our ancestors' land.

If you have never graced the streets of the Crescent City just to roam,
it is a melting pot, of food, art, culture, music and history, I am proud to call home!

RELIGION

The Crescent City is a spiritual melting pot indeed.

It has diverse denominations, rituals, concepts, sub-cultures and creeds.

Some are intrigued by the concept of Voodoo, are true
Protestants, die hard Catholics, or many others.

As an unabridged city, we all appreciate the fervent prayers of our dear grandmothers.

We pay homage to prior generations, who labored and paved the way.

Standing on the shoulders of our dear Madea, who taught us how to pray.

Regardless of manner in which you learned to pray,

you had a preconceived notion, that a higher power guided you each day.

CHILDHOOD MEMORIES

Reminiscent nostalgia of simple things that brought us joy,

the sheer innocence of childhood, of a girl and a boy.

Some went roller skating, bowling, shot dice or played kickball,

others jumped double dutch, hopscotch, rode bikes or strolled the mall.

We attended the World's Fair (1984), the Super Fair and crawfish boils on the lake,

rode the streetcar, visited the Trolley Stop, Audubon Zoo and
the events at the Municipal Auditorium were great.

The city had a plethora of hidden gems, and also obvious things to do,

it was like being a kid at the French Market, or a visitor's dream come true!

REP YOUR HOOD

This multifaceted city is comprised of many parts.

Some lived Uptown, Downtown, East bank, West bank, Garden District

and Pontchartrain Park.

People were proud of their block, and guarded it with care.

Most were loyal to their area and friends, for as long as they remained there.
Some were very territorial, and didn't venture out to other parts.

Others caught the bus (RTA), and greeted strangers with a compassionate heart.

Growing up in an apartment, shotgun house, projects,
townhouse or two-story home, you were proud.

Some blocks had minimal activity, and other sections were quite busy and loud.

People loved the communal spirit, whether you rented or owned.

When the street lights came on, it was the signal, that it's time to go home!

FAMILY TIES

Reminiscing about soul food Sundays and wonderful holidays at Grandma's house,

attending Sunday school and church, sitting on the pew quiet as a mouse.

The family dynamics in everyone's home varied indeed,

however, the genealogy of similarities and differences left people intrigued.
Being old school, we were taught to respect all adults,

which included apologizing to elders, even if it wasn't our fault.

From lower class to upper class and variances in between,

families embodied a sense of pride, to ensure living quarters and

children were clean.

New Orleans natives have deep roots, and a lineage that extends far and wide,

some extend across cities, and others nationwide.

Standing on the shoulders of our forefathers who trailblazed the way,

we thank God for the varying family dynamics each and every day!

SCHOOL DAYS

NOLA natives embody a distinct swagger and pride that's cool.
Generations of students attend homecoming, wear
paraphernalia, and boast about their High School.

Whether you matriculated in the private sector, public realm or magnet institution,
your style, persona and pride for your alma mater came into fruition.

Some were academically intriguing, while others were athletically inclined.
Some were popular participants of marching units, while
others gazed quietly from the sidelines.

Regardless of your part, whether large or small, when it was time to
represent your school, you wore your colors proudly, and stood tall.

It doesn't matter if you graduated uptown, downtown, east bank or
west, magnet, public or private school, we were all the best.

When High school ended, hopefully you formed lasting bonds,
that manifested into lifelong friendships and beyond!

NEIGHBORLY CONNECTIONS

From backyard barbeques to front porch waves, we kept an eye out for

the neighbor's home, and monitored the kids playing.

The elders were notorious, for keeping kids in line,

and the parents appreciated them dearly, knowing that things would be fine.

A smile, nod, wave or exchanging pleasantries was the norm.

If you ever visit the crescent city, you might as well conform.

Southern hospitality was engrained, and it was common to do favors.

As a community we were grateful for our good ole neighbors.

CATCH THAT BEAT

The Crescent City is known for birthing music and exhibiting soul.

Ranging from the sultry sounds of jazz, to tunes that are outright bold.

Blaring from any corner in the French

Quarters, you will surely get a treat.

Feeling the rhythmic sounds of the artist,

you will definitely "catch that beat."

Celebratory events are always a great

time, whether it's watching the

Mardi Gras Indians, Zulu Tramps or bouncing to the Second Line!

"Who Dat"

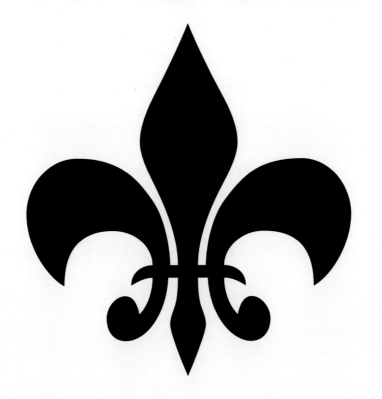

CAJUN----------------------------CREOLE

DIALECT

A cheerful greeting with a highly unique sound, it is recognized world

wide, whenever we come around.

A strong southern drawl, with a mixture of slang,

with a dash of Cajun and Creole, that will drive you insane.

The Crescent City dialect is truly one of a kind,

with variations of endearments, that will blow your mind.

Genuine southern hospitality is definitely shown,

visitors are treated, as if they were our own.

No matter where you migrate or reside, it is a unique flair, that is difficult

to hide.

Whenever we return home, we assimilate well,

it is the only place on earth, where our hearts truly dwell.

GUMBO

NOLA is known for its phenomenal food.

The main reason to convene, and display a good mood.

From shrimp etouffee, jambalaya, or red beans and rice,

to a Tropical Colada, hot sausage po-boy, beignets or crawfish with spice!

There is a flavor to satisfy your palette, regardless of the scene.

The traditions of red beans on Mondays and fried fish on Fridays, and

any delicatessen in between.

If you are in need of a vacation, and undecided what to do, eat, drink and

listen to the music, it's like a dream come true.

ABOUT THE AUTHOR

Natasha is a proud mother of one daughter (Nyah Prier), and a Social Worker. She has a passion for helping people and making connections. She is a native of New Orleans, born to the late Nathaniel and Sarah Thomas. She has two brothers, Byron Thomas and Angelo Riley. Natasha graduated from McDonogh #35 College Preparatory High School. She earned a Bachelor of Science in Psychology, from Southern University and A&M College. She also earned a Master of Social Work degree from Southern University at New Orleans. She is a former member of the National Association of Black Social Workers.

Natasha has a knack for the arts. She is a talented jewelry designer, and dancer since the age of 12. She is also a member of Delta Sigma Theta Sorority Incorporated.

This book captures the essence of New Orleans in poetic form. So, let's take a trip down memory lane, and reminisce about the good times. Hopefully you will enjoy it, as much as I did writing it.

Printed in the United States
By Bookmasters